STEF SMITH

Stef Smith studied Drama and Theatre Arts at Queen Margaret University in Edinburgh.

Stef wrote the text for the critically acclaimed play *RoadKill* (Edinburgh Festival 2010, 2011). The show won a number of awards including a Fringe First, a Herald Angel and the Amnesty International Freedom of Expression Award. In 2012, *RoadKill* transferred to Theatre Royal Stratford East and subsequently won the Olivier Award for Outstanding Achievement in an Affiliate Theatre and then toured to Paris, Chicago and New York.

Stef's previous work for young people includes *Grey Matter* (Lemon Tree, Aberdeen).

Other credits include: *And the Beat Goes On* (Random Accomplice/Perth Horsecross Theatres & Scottish tour); *CURED* (Glasgay!); *Smoke (and Mirrors)* (Theatre Uncut); *Woman of the Year* (Òran Mór); *The Silence of Bees*, *Falling/Flying* (The Tron, Glasgow) and *Tea and Symmetry* (BBC Radio Drama Scotland).

Stef has also been on attachment with the National Theatre of Scotland, an invited residency at the Banff Centre in Canada and is currently under commission at the Royal Court in London. Her play *Swallow* received its world premiere at the Traverse Theatre in Edinburgh in 2015.

Stef Smith

REMOTE

NICK HERN BOOKS

London

www.nickhernbooks.co.uk

A Nick Hern Book

Remote first published as a single edition paperback in Great Britain in 2015 by Nick Hern Books Limited, The Glasshouse, 49a Goldhawk Road, London W12 8QP

Remote copyright © 2015 Stef Smith

Stef Smith has asserted her right to be identified as the author of this work

Cover image: www.istockphoto.com/muansimte

Designed and typeset by Nick Hern Books, London
Printed and bound in Great Britain by CPI Group (UK) Ltd

A CIP catalogue record for this book is available from the British Library

ISBN 978 1 84842 505 7

Remote was commissioned as part of the 2015 National Theatre Connections Festival and premiered by youth theatres across the UK, including a performance at the National Theatre in July 2015.

Each year the National Theatre asks ten writers to create new plays to be performed by young theatre companies all over the country. From Scotland to Cornwall and Northern Ireland to Norfolk, Connections celebrates great new writing for the stage – and the energy, commitment and talent of young theatre-makers.

www.nationaltheatre.org.uk/connections

Thanks

I would like to thank Anthony Banks, Oliver Emanuel, Johnny McKnight, Gilly Roche, Ros & Simon, Davina Shah and all who make NT Connections possible.

With special thanks to Mari Binnie who ran the youth-theatre group I attended as a teenager. Youth theatre emboldened me and made me passionate about theatre, I'm forever thankful for her support and inspiration in those early years.

S.S.

For my parents

8

Characters

ANTLER, *female*
OIL, *male*
CRYSTAL, *female*
BLISTER, *male*
SKIN, *female*
FINN, *female*
DESK, *either gender – he has currently been written as a male
    but if this character is played by a female, the production
    simply changes the gendered pronouns in the [square
    brackets] to female.*
DASHED LINES (–), *any gender/number of performers
    (minimum of two)*
BLISTER'S CREW, *they have no lines but should be
    represented on stage when Blister is in a scene – until they
    disband halfway through the play. If it is a small cast the
    representation of this group does not need to be naturalistic
    but it should give a similar sensation of an ominous group of
    young people.*

*The characters can be any age. The only suggestion is that
Blister appears to be the oldest and Desk the youngest.*

Notes for Production

The smallest number of performers this play could be performed with is nine. There is, however, no maximum number due to the use of a chorus.

The lines denoted with a dash (–) can be said by any performer.

Lines may also be altered, where appropriate, to suit the dialect of the performers. References to high school can also be changed to college, if needed.

This play can be set in any park. The staging can be simple or complex and is open to the interpretation of the group. There are no scenes, but rather this play is one long moment, one long breath, that flicks between the different characters.

Ultimately, the writer wishes for the group to imagine their own world within *Remote*.

–	Lock
–	Open
–	Handle
–	Door
–	Push
–	Step. One foot
–	Then the other
–	Onto the front step
–	She closes the door behind her
–	Fresh air hits her face
–	Smell of clouds and cold. All that autumn stuff
–	She pulls out her phone
–	Places it on the second step
–	Lifts up her foot and slams it down
–	Again
–	And again
–	And again
–	Screen. Buttons. Circuit board. Everywhere.
–	That little piece of plastic
–	Broken into smaller pieces of plastic
–	And her chest is suddenly free and full
–	And she stands for a moment
ANTLER	Good riddance.
–	Good riddance she says.

–   And it's one foot in front of the other

–   It sounds like an easy task

–   And most of the time it is

–   And it's steps

–   No, not steps, strong strides

–   Strong strides forward, always facing forward

–   She pulls her hood up over her head

–   But it isn't that cold

–   It's more for like, an atmosphere

–   A mood

–   Determined.

–   Yeah, a mood best described as determined.

ANTLER   I've got somewhere I need to be. Simple as.

–   The park, mostly it's the park she needs to be at

–   It's only a few minutes' walk from her home

–   Her parents' home.

–   She used to come here often

–   When she was a kid

–   Swings and roundabouts. All that kid stuff.

–   Tarmac and iron

–   Faded painted

–   Mums with prams

–   Eight-year-olds with adventure in their blood

–   The rest of the world ahead of them

–   Tarmac and iron

ANTLER   Huh. It looks the same as it ever did.

–   She steps into the park

–	Walking with purpose
–	Like she is listening to loud headphones
–	But she isn't
–	Nothing is blocking those ears
–	Just those heavy thoughts sitting in between them
–	Swirling around her mind like a Magic Eight Ball
–	And in the middle of this park is a tree.
–	A big old rustic-looking one
–	Been there since always
–	Always been there
–	Got names carved into it
–	Chewing gum stuck to it
–	Holds the snow in the winter
–	Back when it used to snow
–	And she stops at the bottom. Looking up.
–	It's been a long time since she looked at it
–	And for a moment she recognises
ANTLER	Nature is pretty cool.
–	And with that thought, she takes one last look behind her
–	The park at eye level
–	And then she reaches for the nearest branch
–	Grabs it and begins her climb
–	Upwards, onwards.
–	Branch after branch
–	Heaving herself up it.
–	One foot then the other

ANTLER   Those gymnastic classes when I was six, are really
           paying off.

–   She climbs amongst the autumn leaves

–   Flakes of orange and brown

–   Falling like snowflakes

–   Like back when it used to snow

–   She finds a branch, solid and strong

–   She has never been good with heights

–   But then she has never been bad with them either.

–   Breathe hard

–   Breathe deep

–   Taller now.

–   The height of a second-floor window maybe

–   Maybe even third

–   No other trees about here, not any more.

–   This tree stands alone.

–   Surrounded by a world of cars and street lamps

–   Of tall buildings and people talking

–   Of coasts and cliffs

–   Surrounded by this country

–   A piece of land

–   And after all a piece of land is only a piece of land

–   And she shouts

ANTLER   My name is Antler. And I will not be part of the
           world. Not this world. Not any more.

–   And so we cut to the other side of the park

–   A boy called Oil takes his phone out of his pocket

–   Three bars of reception

–	No new calls
–	He shuffles from foot to foot
–	Got new trainers for his birthday
–	They look pretty good but don't fit quite right
–	Clicks contacts
–	Clicks call
OIL	Pick up.
–	His phone does a double ring
–	Goes to voicemail.
OIL	Hey, Antler, it's Oil. Where you at? I got your weird text. What's up with you? Where in the park are you? Why the park? Anyway. I'm out. Call me back.
–	Somewhere not far from here a girl knocks on her sister's door
CRYSTAL	Antler – you in? I'm coming in.
–	But there is no one there. Not a note. Not a sign. Not a nothing.
–	Just a well-made bed and a weirdly tidy room
–	She pulls out her phone.
–	Compose new message
CRYSTAL	Yo. Sis, exclamation mark. Mum says you're to get washing-up liquid from the shop. You out, question mark. Crystal, kiss. Face with its tongue sticking out.
–	Checks her phone again. Nothing.
–	She grabs her jacket
–	Opens the front door
–	Crunch
CRYSTAL	What was that?

–	Broken pieces of plastic
–	Smashed screen
–	Tiny pieces of circuit board
CRYSTAL	Antler's phone.
–	Back in the park a group of shrugs and sighs collect
–	Checking pockets
–	Looking in their bags
SKIN	Nobody got any cigarettes?
BLISTER	What about cash?

The whole group shakes their head and pats their pockets.

SKIN	Nothing.
BLISTER	You lot are worse than useless. Well. We better go find some then.
–	Antler sits. In silence.
–	Looking out for change
–	Listening out for change
DESK	What you doing up there?
ANTLER	What?
DESK	I said what you doing up there?
ANTLER	I'm thinking.
DESK	Can't you just think down here?
ANTLER	Can you leave me alone please?
DESK	It's dangerous being up there so high. At least without ropes. I mean, if you had ropes it would definitely be more safe. But you don't have ropes, so it really isn't safe. I'm Desk. Who are you?
ANTLER	Your name is Desk?
DESK	Sure.
ANTLER	Weird name.

DESK	What's your name?
ANTLER	Antler.
DESK	Antler? Why you called Antler?
ANTLER	It's a long story.
DESK	Have you got somewhere else to be?
ANTLER	Can you just go. I'm having a private moment here.
DESK	I'll go once you tell me.
ANTLER	Why are you called Desk?
DESK	Because it's my name.
ANTLER	Not much of a name is it?
DESK	Works for me.
–	[He] looks up at her
–	She looks down at [him]
–	They pause in that moment
ANTLER	What? Stop watching me. Just move along.
DESK	You just seem a little old for climbing trees.
ANTLER	No age limit on climbing trees – is there? No age limit at all.
DESK	How long are you staying up there?
–	Antler doesn't know how to answer that question
–	Not yet
–	Images of screeching cars
–	And flags in the air
–	And police throwing gas canisters
–	And homeless people
–	And exam results
–	All flick through her head

ANTLER   It's a protest. You're not meant to know how long
           a protest is.

DESK   A protest?

ANTLER   Yeah.

DESK   Have you just decided that?

ANTLER   No.

DESK   What's it about then?

ANTLER   It's private.

DESK   I don't think protests are meant to be private.

ANTLER   Well, this one is.

DESK   Shouldn't people know why you are protesting so
           they know what it is you want done?

ANTLER   It's not that kind of protest.

DESK   Don't you want something done? Like something
           changed or fixed?

ANTLER   Yes.

DESK   Well. What is it then?

ANTLER   How many times do I need to say it's private.

DESK   I don't think you're very good at protesting.

ANTLER   And I don't think you're very good at listening.
           This has nothing to do with you.

DESK   Can I come up then?

ANTLER   Look. I am sorry but go find something else to
           climb.

DESK   Well. You don't own the tree. No one can own
           trees. They're just, there.

ANTLER   Yeah? So?

DESK   So I'm coming up.

–   [He] tries to put one hand on the branch.

–	Lifts [himself] up
–	The branch snaps
DESK	*Merde!*
ANTLER	What?
DESK	Means 'shit' in French.
ANTLER	Well, get you.
DESK	Can you help me up?
ANTLER	I'm doing this solo, kid.
DESK	Is there a nice view? I'd like to see.
ANTLER	You can see the whole park from up here. I mean, sure. It's pretty.
DESK	Can you help me up?
ANTLER	Sorry but there is only room for one up here. Only room for me.
–	The wind whips around them both
–	It's suddenly very cold where Antler stands on the branch.
DESK	It's a giant tree. There must be room for me.
ANTLER	You should go home now. Your mum or legal guardian or whatever will be worried.
DESK	What about your mum?

ANTLER *sits down on the branch.*

–	Antler cuts Desk in half just by looking at [him]
DESK	I best be going. (*Joking.*) Same time, same place tomorrow?
ANTLER	Bye.
–	The [boy] zips up [his] jacket
–	Takes one last look at the girl in the tree
DESK	You're bonkers you are.

ANTLER	See you later Chair.
DESK	It's Desk. My name is Desk.
–	Just north-west from here a boy called Oil also zips up his coat.
OIL	Freaking freezing.
	Checks his phone again. Nothing.
–	His mum says he is addicted to checking his phone
–	But he isn't
–	He can stop any time he wants
–	And he is starting to feel a fizz in his throat
	OIL *bites his nails.*
–	Oil can taste blood in his mouth
–	He chews his fingers till they bleed
–	He never used to
–	He just started doing it this year
–	And now he can't seem to stop
OIL	Just call me back.
–	Just as he says that
OIL	Aw crap.
–	A herd of chants and chewing gum arrive
BLISTER	Oh! Oil-spill. Where is your girlfriend at? Not like your mum to let you out alone.
OIL	Hi, Blister.
BLISTER	What you got for me then?
OIL	Excuse me?
BLISTER	Can I borrow a fiver?
SKIN	Better give him a fiver.

–	This girl called Skin chips in.
–	She might be Blister's cousin but no one is sure and no one dare ask
OIL	I'm still waiting on that fiver you borrowed last week.
BLISTER	I spent it. Need another lend.
SKIN	He needs another fiver.
BLISTER	Anyway the price of smokes has gone up. Inflation, or something.
–	Blister didn't know what inflation meant but it didn't matter
–	He looked much older than his age
–	This was due to a mixture of smoking
–	And wearing jackets that were three sizes too big
BLISTER	Me and my friends here, are desperate for a smoke. We get in a real bad mood if we don't have a smoke after a hard day.
SKIN	And it's been a real hard day.
BLISTER	Really hard.
SKIN	Really really hard.
–	Blister has a gaggle of groupies who follow him around.
–	None of them say much
–	Minus the occasional shout of something about someone's mother
OIL	I haven't got any money, Blister. I only got my phone on me.
BLISTER	Well, then give us that. I'm in need of a new phone, about time I got an upgrade.
SKIN	You heard the big guy.

OIL	You're joking?
BLISTER	Do I look like a comedian?
OIL	I mean, you're funny-looking /
SKIN	/ What did you say?
BLISTER	Phone.
OIL	I got it for my birthday. My mum forked out a fortune.
SKIN	'My mum forked out a fortune.' Whatever.
BLISTER	Now it's your present to me.
OIL	No. I'm not giving you my phone.
BLISTER	What did you say?
OIL	What I'm saying is I'm not giving you my phone.
BLISTER	You want to rethink that?
SKIN	You're probably gonna want to rethink it.
OIL	Why? What are you going to do?
BLISTER	Why don't you imagine what we'll do and then times that by a hundred.
OIL	Why can't you times it by a hundred yourself?
BLISTER	I'm dyslexic.
OIL	No you're just dumb and there *is* a difference.
BLISTER	What did you say?
OIL	I mean, what I meant is…
SKIN	Do you want to repeat that for us? Oil-slick.
–	At this point the group is silent.
–	Blister clenches his fists
–	Skin doesn't blink
–	And Oil just felt his stomach do a high kick into his throat

–	He instantly regretted everything he just said.
–	Oil had a problem with opening his mouth and just letting the words fall out
OIL	Look. Blister. I'm sorry. I'm just messing. I didn't mean to say those things… I'm waiting on Antler calling and I've got all uptight is all.
BLISTER	Your girlfriend? You guys going on a date are you?
–	The good thing about Blister is that due to his overuse of Facebook and Twitter, he was distracted easily
–	No thought or person held his attention too tightly
–	And being the oldest of five siblings, Oil knows how to play a distraction to an advantage
OIL	Yeah, something like that. But I mean we're not actually going out.
BLISTER	She'll be angry you're late. For your date.
SKIN	Tut. Tut. Girls don't like lateness.
BLISTER	And she should know. She's a girl.
OIL	You know. You guys are right. I better go… thanks for the advice.
–	And just like that
–	Oil slips around the group
BLISTER	See you around.
SKIN	See you around.
OIL	Yeah see you around.
–	Disaster narrowly averted
–	Oil gnaws at his nails again
–	He dare not look back as the group walks away
–	And Blister shouts
BLISTER	Enjoy your date!

–	And Skin follows up in the distance with
SKIN	'Oil and Antler up a tree, K-I-S-S-I-N-G.'
–	Just as they disappear
–	Oil bumps into this [boy]
–	Walking at the pace of a snail
–	Which is incorrect because snails don't actually walk
–	But still.
–	But still.
–	All the while Antler had been watching Desk
–	Like a bird perched following a mouse
DESK	Sorry.
OIL	Watch where you're going.
DESK	I said sorry.
OIL	Oi. You might want to turn around.
DESK	Why?
OIL	Bunch of idiots around the corner.
DESK	That's okay. I can look after myself.
–	From high up in that tree in the middle of the park
–	A voice yells
ANTLER	Oil!
–	She shouts it loudly but she is too far up
–	And he is too far away
–	From down here she just sounds like birds
–	Or the wind
–	Or a car in the distance
OIL	It's your life.
DESK	Thanks anyway.

OIL	Whatever.
–	The two of them collide only for a moment
–	And pace off in different directions
–	Meanwhile, Crystal paces the street near her home
–	She doesn't want to tell her mum, doesn't want to get Antler in trouble
–	Even though she knows something has happened
–	Meanwhile, Oil paces the paths of the park
–	I mean, it isn't that big but if someone wants to get lost
–	There is always some way to get lost
–	Meanwhile, Antler sits in the tree. Colder now.
–	Staring across the skyline.
–	She whispers to herself
ANTLER	My name is Antler and I won't be part of this world. Not any more.
–	But there is a slight crack in her voice
–	As if from seeing her friend
–	She isn't so sure any more
–	Her strength loosens
ANTLER	It's fine. I'm fine. You're doing this for a reason. You're doing this for a reason.
–	And she is fine
–	As she thinks about earthquakes
–	And flooding
–	And fires tearing down forests
–	And she looks back up at the sky
BLISTER	Oi! You.
CRYSTAL	What do you want?

BLISTER   We saw your sister's boyfriend kicking about the park – (*Sarcastic*.) bet you're jealous of her getting a stud like him.

CRYSTAL   You saw Oil?

BLISTER   You jealous?

CRYSTAL   No, I'm looking for Antler.

BLISTER   Well, we haven't seen her.

SKIN   Seen nothing of her.

BLISTER   She's probably sucking the face off that numbnut Oil. I mean, they really suit each other. Both total losers.

CRYSTAL   Which way did he go?

BLISTER   Round that way, in past the swings.

SKIN   Off on his date.

CRYSTAL   Right. Thanks.

            With that CRYSTAL *goes to walk past* BLISTER *but he grabs her by her arm.*

BLISTER   Now. Now. We need payment for that information. That information wasn't free of charge.

SKIN   No free passes here.

CRYSTAL   I haven't got any money.

SKIN   She says she hasn't got any money, Blister.

BLISTER   Tut. Tut.

–   He twists her arm

–   Everything closes in

–   Blister can be real brutal when he wants to be

–   Everyone knew that

–   Crystal's arm burned

–   And Blister's eyes lit up

CRYSTAL   That hurts!

BLISTER   You've gotta have something.

SKIN   Someone always has something.

CRYSTAL   I don't have nothing. You're hurting my arm.

FINN   Careful. That's a girl you're hurting.

           BLISTER *lets go of* CRYSTAL*'s arm.*

–   What was that?

–   Who said that?

–   No one, especially not those in this group,
           question what Blister is doing

–   Not on Blister's watch

BLISTER   What did you say?

FINN   It's just not...

SKIN   Tiger got your tongue?

FINN   It's just manners!

BLISTER   Since when have you cared about manners?

FINN   You always said manners are important.

BLISTER   Right. But it isn't manner-ful to question what I
           am doing

SKIN   The man has a point.

FINN   She's younger than you and a girl. She didn't do
           anything. No disrespect /

BLISTER   / No disrespect?

SKIN   You got an eye for her?

FINN   What?

BLISTER   Do you fancy her?

FINN   No. No! It's just... I've got a little sister about her
           age. It's like you're doing it to my sister.

BLISTER   But I'm not.

SKIN   But he isn't.

FINN   But it's like you are. I'm sorry, Blister, but you just gotta be… you know… when it's a girl… I think…

SKIN   Not so mouthy now – are you?

BLISTER   Did I open this up for discussion? For a big chit-chat about manners? Or was I just after some money so I could buy you some fags? Shut up, Finn. Or you can see what happens when someone really has no manners.

For a moment there is silence.

–   This girl called Finn, never said anything to anybody

–   But when she imagined her sister being there

–   Blister with his big hand around her little arm

–   Finn didn't like imagining that

–   She didn't think it was manners at all.

–   And all the while, Antler was watching

ANTLER   Don't you dare hurt her!

–   It was too far to hear them

–   Too far to see the details.

–   And she had no idea what to do

ANTLER   I said don't you dare hurt her!

–   But she was shouting into the air

–   And she couldn't help but feel totally powerless.

FINN   I'm outta here. See you guys later.

BLISTER *grabs* FINN*'s jacket.*

BLISTER   Where do you think you're going?

SKIN	Have you suddenly got somewhere else to be?
–	And just like that all the sides change
–	Friendships, allies, enemies, unknowns, the powerful, the voiceless
–	Everything changes
SKIN	Go on then.
FINN	Go on what?
–	Suddenly, Finn sees a part of Skin that she has never seen before.
–	Eyes close in on her
–	Like a predator
–	Tigers
–	Lions
–	Panthers
BLISTER	Run.
FINN	What?
SKIN	He said run.
FINN	Blister. Don't be a /
BLISTER	/ You turned on us.
SKIN	Now we're turning on you.
–	So quickly, everything switches
–	But no one said any of this would be fair
–	No one said anything about fairness
–	Finn's nerves make her taste sick
–	And her guts make her heart race
	And with that she grabs CRYSTAL*'s hand.*
FINN	Come on!
–	One foot in front of the other

–	One foot in front of the other
–	Blister and his sidestepping crew just stand there
–	Watching
–	Cruelly giving them time to run into the park
–	And up that tree Antler is suddenly starting to feel very stupid
–	She is suddenly starting to feel very pointless
–	I mean, if she got down
–	No one would have to know she was ever there
BLISTER	What do you think fellas? Time to set off after them?
SKIN	I say we give the little puppies a head start. You know. I never... really... well... trusted her.
BLISTER	Oh yeah? What did she do to you?
SKIN	I just never had a good feeling about her. You know that way? When your gut twists?
BLISTER	No. But, yeah.
SKIN	Right. That's enough time, let's head after them.
BLISTER	You calling the shots now?
SKIN	No. Of course not. I'm not calling the shots... I'm just doing as you would do. Aren't I?
BLISTER	Yeah. Yeah. We better go after them.
–	The heavy footsteps of Blister trail off into the park
–	I don't think I like him much
–	I think that's the point
ANTLER	Keep running!
–	Panicked, Antler is stuck
–	She thought it would be easy
–	Easy to stay up in the clouds

–	But she forgot stuff would keep on happening on the ground
–	She hadn't really thought this all through
–	If you ask me, it's a stupid thing to do
–	But she's done it, hasn't she.
–	I mean, no one would have to know she was up there at all
–	She just has to step down off the tree
DESK	You coming down then?
ANTLER	What? No. No... I'm just... Why are you back?
DESK	I've lost a glove. It was in my pocket and now it's not. My mum is gonna be as mad as a bag of cats if she knows I lost a glove. She says I go through gloves like dogs go through bones. Which, if you ask me, is a weird thing to compare it with. Because I don't eat the gloves... I just lose them. So you given up on your protest? It didn't last very long did it?
ANTLER	No I haven't... I wasn't... I'm just getting comfortable.
DESK	It's more comfortable down here. I can promise you.
–	Antler feels a wash of embarrassment over her
–	She didn't want to seem so weak
–	Because this wasn't a phase
–	All of this – it wasn't just a phase
–	It was delayed buses
–	And milk prices
–	And the age of consent
–	It wasn't just a phase
ANTLER	Did you see a group of guys messing with a girl?

DESK   What?

ANTLER   A guy called Blister. Face like a bag of smashed crabs.

DESK   Blister? Why is he called Blister?

ANTLER   Back in primary he gave this boy a Chinese burn so bad it blistered his arm. Name stuck like chewing gum on new Converse. You should stay away from him. He'd eat you alive.

DESK   Well, I haven't seen them. How come?

ANTLER   You see it's just my little sister is... never mind.

DESK   Your little sister what?

ANTLER   It doesn't matter.

DESK   Don't suppose you can see it from up there?

ANTLER   What?

DESK   My glove.

ANTLER   Your glove?! No. I've got more important things to see than your glove.

DESK   Well. It's important to me and that means it is important.

ANTLER   Why care so much? It's only a glove. Go to the corner shop, get sixteen of them for a quid.

DESK   I don't have that kind of money.

ANTLER   You don't have a pound to buy some gloves?

DESK   No.

ANTLER   Just ask your mum then. It's only a quid. You shouldn't stress the small stuff. Plenty of big stuff to be stressing about.

DESK   My mum doesn't have that type of money.

ANTLER   Yeah right. She doesn't have a pound? Whatever.

DESK   She doesn't work.

ANTLER	Then you should get a job.
DESK	How am I supposed to get a job?
ANTLER	Do I look like a careers adviser?
DESK	I don't have time for a job. I look after her.
ANTLER	Oh.
–	With that, Antler delves into her pocket.
ANTLER	Here. Catch.
–	She throws down a pound coin
–	Which was nice of her
–	I think we'd all agree that was a nice thing to do
ANTLER	You can buy a new glove with that.
DESK	Really?
ANTLER	Don't look at me like that. I'll give you another pound if it makes you go away.
DESK	No. You don't have to… Thanks. For the loan.
ANTLER	You don't have to pay me back. I don't need your life story either. Just move along.
DESK	If you ever need… a pal.
ANTLER	I don't need another friend. I don't need anything from *you*. Best be moving, yeah? Why don't you go and see if you can find that other glove… keep the pound for something else.
DESK	Yeah. Yeah. Good idea. See you. I'll give the pound back if I find it.
ANTLER	Whatever. See you.
–	Desk wanders off with [his] eyes to the ground
–	Looking for [his] lost glove
–	And Antler looks back but she can't see her sister
–	Can't see Blister

–   Just the sky slowly turning dark

–   And her stomach grumbles

–   And her teeth grind

–   Listening out for her sister

–   Listening out for change

CRYSTAL   What was that?

FINN   Hey I helped you.

CRYSTAL   He wasn't going to hurt me. Not like, really hurt
           me.

FINN   You don't know him. I've seen him pin kids up to
           walls and turn them upside down.

CRYSTAL   Then why hang out with such a /

FINN   / Protection. You know how in the ocean little fish
           hang out with big fish so they don't get eaten.

CRYSTAL   No.

FINN   Well, they do. That's what I'm doing. I know I'm
           a little fish. Just trying not to get eaten.

CRYSTAL   Sounds like you're being a coward.

FINN   Would a coward do that?

CRYSTAL   It's not like you saved me.

FINN   You looked like you needed saving.

CRYSTAL   I was fine. I would have been fine.

FINN   I was just... I've seen enough folk get ploughed
           through. Between Blister and then there's my
           brothers... well... you get bored of watching
           people get hurt. It gets boring after a while.

–   Unexpected

–   That's the word you'd use for right now

–   Unexpected

CRYSTAL   What's your name?

FINN   Finn.

CRYSTAL   I'm Crystal. You don't go to my school, do you?

FINN   I don't go to any school.

CRYSTAL   Oh yeah?

FINN   Nah. Don't see the point.

CRYSTAL   Oh you're right. Hanging out with Blister is a
                much better plan.

FINN   Better than nothing. In fact, in my life it's better
                than anything else.

–   Both of them stood there

–   Knowing nothing and everything about each other

CRYSTAL   What's your plan then? They just gonna chase us
                around the park for ever?

FINN   They'll get bored soon. We just gotta stay one step
                ahead. That's all. You coming?

–   Just like that, Crystal takes Finn's hand

–   Crystal realises in that moment she hasn't held
                anyone's hand since she was a kid

–   Like, really a kid, younger than now

–   She takes it and they walk further into the park.

–   Crystal likes the small fish, so it seems.

–   And small hands. She realises Finn has
                remarkably small hands.

ANTLER   What am I doing…

–   Now Antler was starting to think about this choice
                she had made

–   It seemed like a simple choice

–   A choice of strength

–   A choice of courage

–   But now she wasn't so sure

–	To be honest I'm not entirely sure either
–	Maybe she was too old for this
–	Because she wasn't a little kid any more
–	She wasn't a child any more
–	The world had made it very clear there was nothing childish about her
–	Exams
–	Pounds
–	Euros
–	Holidays with just friends
–	Saving up for a flat
–	Saving up for a car
–	When you turn old enough
–	But just maybe, this was a rash thing to do
–	I mean, what teenager sits up a tree?
–	All of a sudden it felt like a childish thing to do
–	A grown woman wouldn't do this
–	Would they?
OIL	Pick up your phone.
–	Oil's walked half the park
–	Can't see his friend
–	Can't call his friend
OIL	Look, Antler, it's Oil. Has your phone ran out of charge? I mean. I know there is no point in leaving this voicemail if your phone's died but I mean… if it hasn't and you get this. Can you call me back? I'm waiting for you. It's not cool to leave me just waiting… Hope everything is alright. Call me.
–	Somewhere else in the park, feet are shuffling the leaves

–	Eyes focused on the pavement
–	Sunken into thought
DESK	Excuse me? I was wondering if any of you guys had seen a glove.
BLISTER	A glove?
DESK	Yeah it looks like this one, because it's a pair. You know?
SKIN	Do we look like we've seen a glove?
DESK	I don't know... what does someone look like when they've seen a glove?
–	Silence falls on the group
–	All of them a bit confused by Desk's distinct lack of fear
–	I mean, let's face it, they aren't the sharpest pencils in the pencil case
BLISTER	Where you going?
SKIN	Did you hear him? Where you going?
DESK	I'm just looking for my glove.
BLISTER	Where you been?
SKIN	Where you been?
DESK	Just in the park...
BLISTER	Bit old for parks.
SKIN	Yeah, bit old.
DESK	Do you have to repeat everything he says?
SKIN	No. I can say what I want.
DESK	Then you should.
SKIN	What?
DESK	Say what you want.
SKIN	I do.

DESK   Good.

BLISTER   Hold on what is happening here?

DESK   Nothing. Excuse me...

SKIN   Hey wait. We are looking for these two girls, they
            were running that way.

DESK   I've seen a girl up a tree but not two girls running.

BLISTER   Girl up the tree?

DESK   Sure. The tree up the top of the park.

–   Like a mouse who walks through an alleyway
            filled with stray cats

–   Desk disappears

DESK   Thanks anyway.

BLISTER   What do you say we go and help that girl down?

SKIN   What is that supposed to mean?

BLISTER   Well... From up by the tree we can see the whole
            park. Might be able to spot your friend.

SKIN   She isn't my friend.

–   Doesn't sound good does it?

–   I'm with you on that.

ANTLER   It's fine. I'm fine. Buck. Up. Get yourself together.

–   Antler knew it wasn't madness

–   She knew it came from deep inside her

–   But she also knew somewhere in that park her
            sister was looking for her

–   And she missed Oil.

–   Missed his jokes

–   It was that familiar balancing act of what your
            skull wants

–   And what your ribcage wants

–	Caught in between what came before
–	And what comes next
ANTLER	Another sixty years?
–	If she doesn't smoke or take up an extreme sport
–	She's got another sixty years of this
–	And that was the problem
CRYSTAL	Is it true what they say about Blister?
FINN	About what?
CRYSTAL	About those pills. At that house party.
FINN	Dunno. Depends what people are saying. It's more his big brother's thing.
CRYSTAL	Is it your thing?
FINN	I mean… not really. Why?
CRYSTAL	Just wondering.
FINN	Is it your thing?
CRYSTAL	Are you kidding? My big sister would kill me if I went anywhere near anything like that. She's all protective of me.
FINN	There is no way I'd let my family run my life.
CRYSTAL	You don't know my big sister. And I'd rather take her advice than your best friend Blister.
FINN	Can you just drop all that Blister stuff… He isn't really a friend. Like, not any more.
CRYSTAL	Then why bother? You'd be better off just locking yourself indoors than hanging out with him.
–	What Finn wanted to say is that she had been stuck with them
–	For two years she had stood at the back of that crew
–	But they had been there when her mum kicked her out for a night

–	Or that time that her brothers took her wallet
–	But she had grown up quicker than them.
–	More than them
–	But it was better to have them than no one, she thought
FINN	You know they're not that bad, just immature.
–	Even Crystal knew that wasn't the truth
SKIN	This is taking too long. They'll be out of here before we get halfway to them.
BLISTER	Just go home. The rest of you. Just split.
–	The group pause and look at Blister
SKIN	Yeah. He's right. We can do this alone. We don't need your dead weight.
BLISTER	Alright, Skin. Cool it. No need to get nasty on the ones who do stick around... but yeah. The rest of you can split. We'll see you tomorrow. And bring cash. No empty pockets tomorrow. Unless you want another day without fags.
–	Just like that, the group starts to fade away
–	Nobody else wanted to chase two girls around the park
–	Nobody else really cared
BLISTER	Just us then.
SKIN	Looks like it.
–	Antler can see this.
–	She sees the group break up.
–	She could feel sweat in her palms
–	Could feel her eyes twitch
–	Everything had switched
–	And she had no idea what to do

ANTLER   Screw this.

–   It's so much harder than she thought it would be

–   Because no one had warned her how hard it would be to change

SKIN   You should be worried, Blister. Finn leaving us. Don't want anyone else getting ideas, you know. Ideas like that can be contagious. Can be poison. When people get busy making their own ideas of how things should be, well, that's when it gets dangerous for big fish like us.

BLISTER   Big fish? I'm allergic to fish.

SKIN   Big tigers. Lions. Whatever. You know back in the day there would have been wolves here. And that's us. We're the wolves now. And it's important people know that.

BLISTER   I thought there used to be a Tesco here?

SKIN   Before that. Before all the humans. Wolves have real sharp teeth. And they aren't afraid to use them.

BLISTER   I've never been afraid, Skin. Even with everything that's happened, I've never been afraid.

SKIN   That's why you're my friend, Blister. That's why all that lot, respect you.

BLISTER   Yeah. Yeah you're right. Better go then.

SKIN   You lead the way.

–   And with that, Skin could hear her brother's voice ring in her head

–   Protect yourself

–   The world is filled with wolves

–   Protect yourself

OIL   You have got to be kidding me. Antler? Is that really you?

–   The two of them just look at each other

–   Connected in silence and confusion

OIL   What are you doing up there? You hate climbing trees.

ANTLER   Oil, you gotta go after Crystal. Blister is after her.

OIL   What?

ANTLER   You gotta go.

OIL   What's wrong with your legs?

ANTLER   I can't come down, Oil.

OIL   Are you stuck?

ANTLER   No... I just... /

OIL   / I tried calling you.

ANTLER   I smashed my phone up.

OIL   What?!

ANTLER   Don't need it.

OIL   You don't need it?

ANTLER   I don't need it.

OIL   You're not going to /

ANTLER   / Not any more.

OIL   Not any more?

ANTLER   Is there an echo? Look can you just go and check and see if Crystal's okay?

OIL   Why don't you come down and we can go and look together?

–   No words found Antler

–   She felt this strange double feeling of shame and strength

–   And her mind flicked to news broadcasters

–   And trashy magazines

–   And size zero

–   And kissing boys

–	And not kissing boys
–	And definitely not getting pregnant before you're twenty
–	And turning off lights when you leave the room
–	And recycling
–	And all she could mutter out was –
ANTLER	I can't.
OIL	Look. Come on. Enough of this. Let's go see what's happening.

ANTLER *shakes her head.*

Look, I'm not going after Crystal without you. This is stupid. Just get down. Blister is rolling around the park looking for trouble. You want to be up there when he comes?

ANTLER	I don't care if Blister wants me.
OIL	Are you being a hero all of a sudden?
–	The truth is Antler had never felt less like a hero
–	She takes a deep breath
–	Like the kind you take before you dunk your head underwater
ANTLER	I'm not being a 'hero'… but I don't want part of any of it any more.
OIL	Part of what?
ANTLER	Anything. Everything.
OIL	School?
ANTLER	No.
OIL	Something at home?
ANTLER	No. And yes. All of that. All of everything. I mean, take a look around. This… well… It's a protest.
OIL	A protest? Can you have a protest with just one person?

ANTLER   It's a protest against all of that.

–   Both Antler and Oil take their eyes off each other

–   And they look at the ground

–   Look at the sky

–   Look at everything they know

ANTLER   It's all turning to shit.

OIL   I don't... Since when... Can you just come down?

ANTLER   No. Not any more.

OIL   It sounds like you're being a bit... Look. It
           doesn't matter. Come on. Protest on the ground or
           something.

–   Her hands were shaking

–   Her eyes were welling up

ANTLER   Can't you see? Everything matters.

CRYSTAL   Look. Thanks for... well... I dunno... but I'm
           gonna split. I gotta find my sister.

FINN   Just like that? Gone?

CRYSTAL   What do you want?

FINN   I can't leave you to wander off by yourself... you
           don't know where Blister is.

CRYSTAL   It's fine. I don't think he is half as tough as you
           think he is. You've got some idea of him in your
           head. He's just a guy... whatever.

FINN   You kidding? A couple of weeks ago he found this
           little dog. This little three-legged thing. It was old,
           more scabs than fur. Skin pinned the dog down to
           the ground – it was yelping and crying and then
           Blister picked up this big rock and dropped it on
           its head. And it stopped yelping but he didn't stop.
           He just picked up the rock again and smashed it
           into the dog and he smashed and smashed and
           smashed. Until... well, until the dog was nothing.

Skin said it was kinder to put it out its misery but the dog had seemed fine to me. And they just left it there. It's just the other side of the park. And they've still got blood on their shoes. All dried in their laces. I haven't ever seen something like that before... and I don't want to see it again.

CRYSTAL   Why didn't you stop them?

FINN   What was I supposed to do? When they get their minds on something... I mean, look at us. I'm not gonna just let you go wandering off into the park.

CRYSTAL   I can look after myself.

FINN   I got you into this mess.

CRYSTAL   But I'm not a three-legged dog. I'll be alright.

Honest.

Silence.

FINN   That boy you were looking for.

CRYSTAL   Oil?

FINN   Yeah. He was walking up to the top of the park. Towards the tree.

CRYSTAL   Thanks.

–   And with that she leans forward and kisses her

–   Right on the lips

–   It was a short kiss

–   No tongues

–   Crystal knew she didn't have to be saved but she didn't mind the gesture

–   And both were a little surprised by the kiss

–   But neither were particularly scared

CRYSTAL   See you.

FINN   See you.

–   One foot in front of the other

–	One foot
–	Then the other
–	Different directions
OIL	Look. Come down. We'll find Crystal and sort this out.
ANTLER	How many times do I need to say it?
OIL	Come on. It's getting dark. And I don't have a torch. My phone has ran out of battery, yours is smashed. Your sister could be lost in the park for all we know. It's not just you here! Stop being so stupid. I'm gonna walk away, Antler...
–	The sky dims
–	Clouds move in
–	Right enough, it was getting dark
OIL	Your mum will be worried.
–	It was a cheap shot but it was enough to make Antler's heart jump up to her tongue.
ANTLER	I told her I was staying at yours.
OIL	I'm not sure she'll buy that excuse when you don't come home for a week.
ANTLER	I just can't do it. Not any more. It's too hard. My mum cries. A lot. My room is next to the bathroom and I hear her cry. I don't know why, Oil. She just cries. And you know it isn't good when your mum cries.
OIL	How long has she been crying?
ANTLER	Long enough. And my dad has taken up smoking again.
OIL	So? You smoke at parties.
ANTLER	But it's different. He's quiet. He looks... well... And I hate school. I hate it. I don't care about some revolution that happened eighty years ago.

And there is no way I'm getting in to uni with my grades and it's not like I have the money to move out and I don't have a job and I don't want to be like forty-five and still living with my mum.

Silence.

OIL   Is this all like… a hormone thing… or something?

ANTLER   I'm not on my period, Oil.

OIL   Ew. Gross. Look. Come down. And we can talk about it. I'm getting a right sore neck look up at you and soon you won't be able to see where the branches are, come down. It's just getting dangerous.

ANTLER   Good. Let it get dangerous.

OIL   You got a death wish?

ANTLER   No. But at least something would change. It's just grey. Look at all that grey.

–   And Antler felt a twinge in a muscle just left of her heart

–   As she looked out at the greyness

–   And she knew it wasn't about that stuff

–   Not really.

–   Go on then.

–   Tell him.

ANTLER   That's not really why I'm here. It's just…

OIL   Spit it out.

ANTLER   I learnt a word the other day. In English. She was going on about some old book about something and she said – it was about people being Apathetic… it was about Apathy.

OIL   Oh yeah. What does that mean then?

ANTLER   It's people not caring. People not wanting to care about anything.

OIL   Can you tell me how you sitting up a tree is you
            not caring?

ANTLER   No. That's not the point. After she said the word, I
            saw it everywhere and I can't stop seeing and
            feeling it everywhere. And I don't think that's
            right. People not caring. It's frustrating... it's...
            hard... it's...

OIL   Are you gonna start going on about starving kids?

ANTLER   Stop trying to make it small. This isn't small.
            These thoughts aren't small.

OIL   Look. Sort all that stuff out when we're out of
            high school. Keep it small. It's like a survival
            thing. Just got to keep that kinda thing in the back
            of your mind until you can actually do something
            about it.

ANTLER   What? Like everyone else around us?

OIL   You're not exactly volunteering are you?

ANTLER   No. It's not that!

–   Antler grabs her chest.

–   And tears fill in her eyes but none of them drop

–   She didn't like the world much

–   And she didn't know what to do with that feeling

–   Didn't know where to put it

OIL   Look. Don't get all wrapped up in it. You can save
            the world another day. Just come down. Yeah?

ANTLER   But that's it, isn't it? I can't change the world and
            I definitely can't save it. I can't do nothing.

            Silence.

–   The two friends look at each other

–   Oil started biting his nail again

–   And Antler felt like her lungs might burst

–	It's been years since they fought
–	They might only have been feet away but they felt also worlds away
OIL	What about your sister?
–	Antler felt a double twang of guilt and sadness
ANTLER	I can't come down.
–	I mean, she wanted to come down
–	She wanted to find her sister
–	And shout at her
–	Tell her off
–	And then hug her
–	The way that big sisters do
–	But she didn't
–	She was sitting there, in that tree
–	Wishing for something better
–	Wanting something bigger
–	One foot
–	Then the next
–	Antler looks out at the grey, her eyes wet with wanting
–	Oil looks at his friend and tastes blood in his mouth
–	Skin paces up the hill, looking for wolves, ready to jump
–	Blister walks two steps behind, uncertain of this change of sides
–	Finn touches her lips, thinking of the kiss, wondering how she felt
–	Crystal feels the power in her feet, in her hands

| – | Desk suddenly turns on [his] feet. Suddenly aware that [he's] sent a pack of animals to roar at a girl up a tree... what has [he] done? |

CRYSTAL   Oi! You seen /

OIL   / Crystal! Look your sister won't get down.

ANTLER   You're alright? You're okay!

CRYSTAL   I've been looking for you! I've been worried sick, I've been... What are you doing?

OIL   She won't get down.

ANTLER   I was worried, I could see Blister coming after you. Did he hurt you?

CRYSTAL   How did you know about Blister? What else did you see? Did you see me?

ANTLER   I could see him chasing you.

CRYSTAL   And you didn't come help?

ANTLER   I mean...

OIL   She isn't coming down. She doesn't like the world.

ANTLER   So what happened with Blister? Why was he so mad?

CRYSTAL   Hold the phone! What was that about the world?

–   Antler was lost again

–   Someone new to describe everything to

–   And somehow with these people who she was closest to

–   She found it hardest

–   She found it hardest to explain that ache

–   The ache in her chest, in her skull

CRYSTAL   Is this about those sad adverts on the TV? I told you not to watch them any more.

OIL   I've already asked that – it's not about the sad
              adverts.

CRYSTAL   Is it about school? Home?

OIL   No it's not about that either. But also kinda
              everything.

CRYSTAL   You can't be that upset – we're having a roast for
              dinner, oh and Mum says you're to get washing-
              up liquid.

OIL   Maybe it would help just not paying attention to
              what the TV is saying, yeah? Just like forgetting
              about all of it.

CRYSTAL   This better not be a joke. 'Cause it isn't funny. I
              can't believe I spent all afternoon looking for you
              and you've just been stuck up here. You know
              what, Antler, I don't even care. I'm going home
              with or without. Oil, you coming?

              OIL *looks at* CRYSTAL. *He is tempted. He is*
              turning on his feet.

              Coming?

ANTLER   Just stop it!

–   And in her head it was

–   Images of screeching cars

–   And flags in the air

–   And police throwing gas canisters

–   And homeless people

–   And exam results

–   And earthquakes

–   Flooding

–   Forests on fire

–   Delayed buses

–   Milk prices

–	The age of consent
–	Exams
–	Pounds
–	Euros
–	Holidays with just friends
–	Saving up for a flat
–	Saving up for a car
–	News broadcasters
–	Trashy magazines
–	Size zero
–	Kissing boys
–	Not kissing boys
–	Not getting pregnant before you're twenty
–	Turning off lights when you leave the room
–	And recycling

ANTLER   Recycling!

OIL   What?

CRYSTAL   You're kidding me. Now I really am going.

ANTLER   No. It's not that. But it is that. It's not that simple. There is nothing simple about these thoughts, there is nothing simple about me, or you or this place, this town, this country. And people try to tell you it's easy. Simple. But really it's just that no one cares. No one cares enough to see what it's really like. How *hard* everything is. Because it's hard. It's hard knowing that you can't fix anything. You can't do nothing about anything. It's hard. And no one cares.

            Silence.

CRYSTAL   I care.

ANTLER   You care more about the shape of eyebrows than
          you do about what's happening in the world.

CRYSTAL   That's just mean.

OIL   Why should we care?

ANTLER   Because it's ours as well.

          This is what we'll get. This. Their mess. And I
          don't want it, Oil. I don't want any of it.

          Silence.

–   With that, silence falls on the trio

–   It's painful to see the world

–   Oil understood that now

–   It's painful to see what the world really is.

OIL   Well, hiding up a tree isn't the best way to… fix it.

ANTLER   Then what do you propose?

OIL   I've got no interest in proposing anything. Voting?

ANTLER   Do you think that does anything?

CRYSTAL   (*Sarcastic.*) Oh sure. It's not nearly as useful as
          hiding up a tree.

–   Minutes away, Finn turns on her heels

–   She knows that she's got to see that girl again

–   Minutes away, Skin and Blister march up closer to
          the tree.

–   Seeking out something to stir up, seeking out
          something.

–   Minutes away, Desk runs towards the tree.

–   Wanting to make sure no trouble was caused.

ANTLER   Then what else? I can't think of anything else to do.

CRYSTAL   You're acting like a right idiot. You haven't even
          got a decent reason. I'm gone, I'm so gone.

ANTLER	You're the reason, Crystal! You're the reason I'm up here!
CRYSTAL	It's my fault? Why is it my fault?
ANTLER	I didn't want to tell you because I didn't want to upset you, but...
–	And just like that, everything changed again
FINN	Crystal!
CRYSTAL	Finn? What are you doing...
FINN	I needed to talk to you, about what happened /
OIL	/ What you doing knowing this loser? She's pals with Blister.
CRYSTAL	She isn't like that. She... helped... me earlier.
OIL	Leopard can't change its stripes.
ANTLER	Spots. Leopards have spots.
FINN	I didn't mean anything earlier. Like sorry about your phone and that. Blister was just joking.
OIL	Wasn't very funny.
BLISTER	I thought it was pretty hilarious.
SKIN	Don't mind us, we've got a bit of business needed with our friend here.
OIL	Thought you weren't friends with these guys any more.
BLISTER	No one said anything about friends.
SKIN	I did. I said friend.
BLISTER	Oh.
CRYSTAL	Just leave us alone.
SKIN	Oh we'll go, all in good time.
OIL	You just the sidekick, Blister?
BLISTER	You kidding? I'm still the boss around here.

OIL	Doesn't look like it
SKIN	None of us have any bosses, not any more.
BLISTER	Oi. Skin. Watch your mouth.
FINN	Look, I'm sorry for before. I'm sorry. I was out of line.
CRYSTAL	What are you saying, Finn?
FINN	Look, I've got some money at home. I'll buy your smokes for the rest of the week.
–	Crystal felt the knot of disappointment
–	Blister felt sweat in his palms
–	And Skin just glared at Finn
–	And I have no idea what is going to happen
BLISTER	I think that's fair, Skin. I could do with a smoke. We've all had a stressful day.
SKIN	I don't. I don't think that's a good offer. I'm not soft like you, Blister.
BLISTER	Soft?
FINN	Look. Skin, what happened before, it didn't mean nothing.
–	With that, Skin reaches down
–	She picks up the branch that Desk had snapped off
–	From up above Antler can see
ANTLER	Watch!
	SKIN *swings the branch near* FINN.
FINN	You planning on putting that down?
SKIN	Are you planning on staying still for me?
	SKIN *aims at* FINN.
CRYSTAL	What are doing?!
SKIN	Don't come near me!

BLISTER	This isn't funny. You could mess her up with that.
SKIN	That's the point.
FINN	Look, Skin. I didn't mean nothing. I'm sorry. Alright. No need to do nothing drastic.
SKIN	I know you like to kiss girls. I was doing you a favour, keeping it private. But then today... when I saw run off with her... I think... Well, why I don't I just show you what I think about that.
	SKIN *steps forward. The branch in her arms. Ready to swing.*
–	Now Finn sees the dried blood on Skin's shoes
–	She thinks about that three-legged dog
–	Thinks about what its head looked like after the rock
FINN	Stop! I'm sorry. Okay? I'm sorry. I didn't mean nothing. I kissed a girl. Okay? But I don't know... like... I'm just...
SKIN	Do me a favour and stand still. Will you?
CRYSTAL	We kissed. Alright? Didn't mean nothing. Just a kiss. No need to give someone a decking just for a kiss.
BLISTER	Just put it down, Skin. You hit her with that, you'll get done. You don't want that. Trust me, my brother got put in a unit. And she isn't worth it. She isn't worth it.
–	A tear creeps out of Blister's eye but he quickly wipes it away
–	Oil is pretty sure his heart has stopped
–	And Finn just stares into Skin's eyes.
DESK	Don't hurt her! I won't let you hurt her.
–	Out of nowhere, Desk rushes up to Skin
–	He tries to grab the branch

–   They tug back and forth

–   Skin pushes [him] off

SKIN   Enough! I oughta smash in all your skulls just for being cowards. Look at you. You don't have the guts to fight. You don't have the guts to do nothing about this, me. Scared of a stupid branch?! Bunch of cowards. Don't even know how to fight. You'll get nowhere if you don't know how to fight. You're just a bunch... of kids. Stupid kids, the lot of you.

SKIN *throws the branch on the ground.*

–   They stand there.

–   In silence.

–   Looking less like kids and more like adults by the minute

Silence.

CRYSTAL   I'd rather be a coward than just plain stupid.

CRYSTAL *quickly picks up the branch. She points it at* SKIN *who barely finches.*

BLISTER   Oi! Don't talk to her like that.

–   Skin looks at Blister

–   Relieved to have the responsibility of words taken away from her

–   Blister steps in the middle

He pushes the branch down.

–   No one is getting hurt today, he thinks

–   No one is getting hurt

–   I don't know about you but I'm relieved

–   Shhh!

DESK   What has been happening here?!

Silence.

ANTLER   We're just trying not to fuck it up.

–   One by one they turn and look at the girl in the tree

ANTLER   You're wrong. It isn't about fighting, not in that way. I mean, look at everyone around us. All the power in the world and they don't care about nothing, don't fight for anything. We aren't being cowards by not fighting.

–   It's just about choosing what to fight for.

–   Antler realised that now

–   She did want to fight

–   But she wanted to fight for something better than this

ANTLER   Because when I fight. I want it to be for more than you holding a branch up to some girl because she kissed another girl. Them kissing... what does it matter? If they're happy – that's a good thing. I don't want to fight that. Skin, you're fighting something pointless, something that doesn't need fighting, and I've got better things to do with my time, better things to fight for, we all do.

      Silence.

SKIN   No need for the lecture.

OIL   Antler, it's time to come down... yeah?

CRYSTAL   Hold on. What did you mean I caused you going up there?

–   With deep dark breaths Antler sighs

–   Exhausting

–   Antler knew one thing

–   Change was exhausting

ANTLER   It was that text.

CRYSTAL   Text?

ANTLER   You sent me that message.

CRYSTAL   What message?

ANTLER   I asked you if you wanted to go and see Gran this
            weekend or next and you said – 'I don't care either
            way and I don't need you to organise my life.' You
            typed that into your phone and sent it to me. In
            about thirty seconds. You said you didn't care.
            You said you didn't need me.

–   The group looks amongst themselves

–   No one is quite sure of her point

–   To be honest I don't know her point but I sense
            she probably has one

CRYSTAL   I mean, maybe it was a bit harsh but there is no
            need for all this. I just meant I'm free all
            weekend…

ANTLER   But you said you didn't care. You said you didn't
            need me. And I thought, if my own sister can say
            that. Then it really is messed up.

CRYSTAL   But that's just what sisters do? That's just normal.
            You say stuff like that all the time.

ANTLER   No. I don't. I'm careful with my words.

CRYSTAL   You're older.

ANTLER   Only by a year… It's apathy. It's everywhere. You
            said you didn't care. You said you didn't need me.
            I mean, what can I do? How can I change any of
            this? If I can't get my own sister to care about me.

CRYSTAL   Look. I'm sorry. I was in a bad mood.

FINN   I think you're reading too much in to it.

ANTLER   No. It was like. What's that saying?

BLISTER   The straw that broke the camel's back.

            The whole group turn and look at BLISTER.

            What? I know stuff.

ANTLER   Exactly.

OIL   Is that why you stamped on your phone?

ANTLER   Texting seemed pointless. Facebook seemed
             pointless. Taking another stupid photo of my cat
             seemed pointless. It doesn't matter – does it? Any
             of that stuff.

–   It doesn't matter when there is better stuff to care
             about.

–   That's what she wanted to say

–   That there was bigger stuff to care about.

ANTLER   That stupid phone was just... just... a distraction.

–   It stopped her from seeing the world for what it
             really is.

–   It stopped everything.

–   She saw that now.

DESK   If you ask me, Antler. You're the one who cares
             least... what's that word?

BLISTER   Apathy...

             The group turn and look at BLISTER *again.*

             What? I was paying attention.

DESK   Apathy. Sounds like some weird disease. Us,
             down here, on the ground. We care. We've got no
             choice. Otherwise it's just... boring or pointless or
             whatever. You've got to care about something.
             Everyone knows that. And you're just up there. In
             that tree. It's one thing to count yourself out but it
             just seems stupid to count yourself out because
             others are counting themselves out.

CRYSTAL   What?

DESK   She is doing the exact thing she hates other people
             are doing.

CRYSTAL   Oh. Right.

DESK   I don't know how you fix people not caring. I
             don't know how you get people to notice all the

| | things that need fixing. Because it's everywhere, the stuff that needs fixing. All of us can name three things in thirty seconds that need fixing, but you aren't going to fix it by not being part of it. |

SKIN   Talk about sugar-coating something.

BLISTER   Shut up, Skin.

OIL   What you were saying before? You're right. This is ours. All of this is ours. But we can't make it ours, like truly properly ours, unless we're in it. Can't fix anything by being above it.

–   There are shifts you feel

–   Somewhere under your ribcage

–   Somewhere just left of your heart

–   Something happens

–   Like something changes

–   And it will happen plenty of times over the years

–   Even I know that

–   It's like a breathlessness

–   Yeah, it's best described as a breathlessness.

–   And Antler felt that. As she sat in the tree. Looking down.

–   Looking down at those people

–   People who looked just as confused as she was

–   It had been a hard autumn, she thought.

–   The autumn of what came before, and what comes next.

OIL   Please, come down.

CRYSTAL   I need you. I'm sorry I said I didn't. Like... I was wrong. Simple as. I care. I've always cared.

–   And just like that. It all changes again.

–	Just when you get a hold of something
–	Just when you decide
–	It changes
ANTLER	Alright.
–	An exhale
–	A breath taken
ANTLER	On one condition. You all gotta come up here first.
OIL	What?
ANTLER	It's the sun. It's setting. You can't see it from down there. Too close to the ground. But from up here. The reds and the yellows. It's beautiful.
–	Antler looks at Blister and Skin
ANTLER	But first I think it's best you guys get gone now.
CRYSTAL	You heard her.
–	Blister and Skin look at the group
–	Bunch of no ones
–	Bunch of everyones
BLISTER	We know where we're not wanted. You coming?
–	Finn shakes her head
FINN	Not this time.
SKIN	Best we don't see you again, yeah?
FINN	Yeah.
–	In silence the two march off
–	They won't talk about what happened today
–	Not ever
–	But it changed them
–	In the smallest of ways, it changed them
ANTLER	Look, I promise I'll get down, afterwards. Come on. See this.

–	And just like that
–	One by one they start climbing the tree
–	Helping each other
–	Clambering upwards
CRYSTAL	I don't think I like heights.
FINN	You'll be alright.
–	Branch after branch
–	One foot above the other
–	The group settle in the branches of the tree
–	Like crows
–	Or pigeons
–	Or seagulls
–	Or robins
–	All perched in the branches
–	Watching the light change
–	Watching the sun dip below this big lump of rock
OIL	It's cool how the light changes.
ANTLER	Desk! I can see your glove! Look! Over by there… oh no. It's just a crisp packet.
FINN	Everything looks so much smaller up here.
CRYSTAL	What do they call it? Like, in a photo. We just learnt it in art. All the depth and that…
ANTLER	Perspective.
CRYSTAL	Yeah. Perspective.
–	And then in a single moment
–	A speck of white falls from the sky
–	Antler holds out her hand
–	And catches it and it disappears

–	Was that snow?
–	Antler wasn't sure.
–	But she did know. The sun would most likely rise again.
–	Just as it would set again.
–	It's amazing what you can see if you look.
ANTLER	Nature is pretty cool.
–	As darkness and shadows fall on the group
–	They all sit in silence
–	Hold on to the branches a little tighter
–	And they are still, if only for a moment.
–	Antler smiles to herself as she wonders if the whole day was worth it
–	If it was worth the battle
–	Just so she could see this sunset
–	And she concluded it probably was
–	It was always worth seeing another sunset.
–	She promised herself she'd look up more. So she didn't miss it.
–	Perspective, after all, is everything.
–	With that, Desk broke the settled silence
DESK	Just one thought…
	How are we going to get down?
	Blackout.

www.nickhernbooks.co.uk

facebook.com/nickhernbooks

twitter.com/nickhernbooks